EARTH'S smallest SUPERHEROES

TARDIGRADES

by Ruth Owen

With thanks to:
Dr. Thomas C. Boothby
Associate Professor
Department of Molecular Biology,
University of Wyoming, Laramie, WY, US

Ruby Tuesday Books

Published in 2026 by Ruby Tuesday Books Ltd.

Editor: Mark J. Sachner
Design & Production: Alix Wood

Picture credits:
Alamy: 20T (NASA photo), 22B (Olivier Asselin), 25C (Newscom); ESA: 21T; Ingemar Jönsson: 21B; NASA: 24L; Public Domain: 7TR; Science Photo Library: 6 (Eye of Science), 10 (Eye of Science), 11T (Eye of Science), 11B (Eye of Science), 12B (Steve Gschmeissner), 13T (Eye of Science), 15 (Frank Fox), 22T (Eye of Science); Shutterstock: Cover (Dotted Yeti/3dMediSphere), 1 (TajdidProtik), 4 (Oleh Liubimtsev), 5TL (Olga Moonlight), 5TR (Vadim Sadovski), 5BL (Inked Pixels), 7TL (SpeedKingz), 7B (Anucha Cheechang), 8TL (Teo Tarras), 8TC (Willem Tims), 8TR (Lucky-photographer), 8BL (Joe Barti), 8BR (vixit), 9T (Artem Kniaz), 9CL (Nik Merkulov), 9CR (Seksan44), 9B (Oleh Liubimtsev), 12T (Surakit Sawangchit), 13B (Dotted Yeti), 16T (RachenArt), 16B (WinWin artlab), 17 (Lillac), 17B (3dMediSphere), 18T (Triff), 18B (Gl0ck), 19T (Denis--S), 19BL (Dotted Yeti), 19BR (End_ru99/CG_dmitriy), 23T (MBLifestyle), 23B (Toto Santiko Budi), 24R (Paopano), 26T (J.J. Gouin), 26B (Mark Kostich), 27T (Olena Yakobchuk), 27B (Dotted Yeti), 28T (Triff), 28B (Qasimphotographer), 29 (TajdidProtik); Superstock: Cover (The Science Picture Company); Alix Wood: 14.

Library of Congress Control Number: 2025936405

Print (Hardback) ISBN 978-1-78856-465-6
Print (Paperback) ISBN 978-1-78856-466-3
ePub ISBN 978-1-78856-467-0

Published in Minneapolis, MN
Printed in the United States

www.rubytuesdaybooks.com

Contents

What Is a Tardigrade?

We realize this may not be the most exciting or enticing question with which to begin a book about superheroes.

However, it's the question we get asked the most. So, let's begin. . . .

THIS is a tardigrade.

Tardigrades are also known as moss piglets because of their pig-like snouts.

Kind of weird, but cool. So how many tardigrades are there on Earth?

Good question, but impossible to answer. However, what we do know is that any estimate would include a serious number of zeros. We are talking billions of tardigrades, probably even trillions. . . .

100,000,000,000,000

Still like what I'm hearing. But why are they superheroes?

We're glad you asked!

A group of tardigrades were frozen solid for 30 years—and they survived!

Tardigrades have lived on Earth for more than 540 million years. They even survived the extinction events that killed the dinosaurs and other prehistoric species.

You can put tardigrades into a hot oven, and it won't kill them.

(But please don't try this at home!)

Wow! These guys sound awesome. So how come I've never seen one?

Hello! I'm down here.

Yep! Tardigrades are small. Seriously small.

But whoever said that superheroes have to be large?

Meet a Tardigrade

So tell me. What do I need to know about tardigrades?

Tardigrades are tiny, near-microscopic animals. So far, scientists have discovered about 1,500 different species, or types.

No Bones!

A tardigrade has no bones. It is filled with a liquid that supports its body—a little like a balloon filled with water. The liquid acts like blood, carrying nutrients around the animal's body.

Outer Shell

A tardigrade has a tough, but bendy, shell called a cuticle.

An SEM image of a tardigrade

Some types of tardigrades have hair-like bristles that help them feel and detect information about their world.

Some types of tardigrades are 1 mm long. About 25 of them laid end to end would measure 1 inch (25 mm). Some types are much smaller!

Tardigrades can be seen with a home or classroom light microscope.

Light microscope

Scientists study tardigrades with powerful Scanning Electron Microscopes (SEMs). This type of microscope connects to a computer that creates an on-screen SEM image of the item being studied.

Computer images

Scanning Electron Microscope

Little Water Bear

Tardigrades were first discovered in 1773 by a German scientist named Johann Ephraim Goeze.

Goeze's drawing of a tardigrade

Goeze called them *Kleiner Wasserbär*, because of their slow movements that look like a bear's lumbering walk. The name means "little water bear."

In 1776, an Italian scientist named them *Tardigrada*. It means "slow stepping."

Tardigrades have tiny eye spots that can see light and dark, but not colors.

Planet Tardigrade

So where do these tiny superheroes hang out?

Great question! Tardigrades live in nearly every environment on Earth.

Some of their homes are truly extreme!

Dark, steamy jungles

Freezing Antarctica

Scorching deserts

Tardigrades live near volcanoes and at the bottom of deep oceans. They have even been found in the Himalayas—the highest mountains in the world.

These dangerous worlds would mean instant death to other living things.

Erupting volcano

The Himalayas

Remember their nickname of "moss piglets"? Tardigrades also live in patches of moss that grow in backyards and playgrounds, and on the roofs of buildings. They also live in soil and rotting leaves.

Moss on a roof

A patch of backyard soil the size of a sheet of printer paper may contain 20,000 tardigrades.

A patch of moss the same size will be home to 125,000 tardigrades!

Wherever it lives, a tardigrade must be surrounded by a thin film, or layer, of water. That's because the tiny animal soaks up oxygen from water through its cuticle. Without water, a tardigrade can't breathe.

An illustration of a tardigrade in pond water

A Day in the Life of a Tardigrade

Tardigrades have carried out some daring, superhero missions. But more on that later! So what does a tiny tardigrade do on an average day?

A tardigrade crawls around its habitat, such as some moss in a backyard, looking for food.

As they walk, tardigrades hook their claws into moss or soil.

An SEM image of a tardigrade in moss

Some species of tardigrades feed on moss, algae, and fungi. Others are carnivores that eat microscopic animals—and even other tardigrades!

An SEM image of a tardigrade feeding

A tardigrade uses spear-like mouthparts to pierce its food. Then, just like a tiny vacuum cleaner, it sucks up nutritious juices with its powerful, round snout.

These guys are cute. What else do I need to know?

An SEM image of a tardigrade egg

Tardigrades can reproduce quickly. Some types are ready to have young when they are just 10 days old themselves.

Some types of tardigrades have males and females. They mate and then the female lays eggs.

There are some tardigrade species that are all female. They produce eggs that do not need to be fertilized by a male.

I think I heard somewhere that tardigrades can live forever. Is that true?

Hmmm. . . . Not exactly. . . . They usually live for just a few months. But let's take a look at a tardigrade's number one superhero skill.

The Long Sleep

If the place where a tardigrade lives starts to dry up or freeze solid, the tiny animal is in big trouble!

A pond drying up

Without water, a tardigrade can't breathe and won't survive. To protect its body, the tardigrade curls up inside its cuticle, pulling in its head and legs.

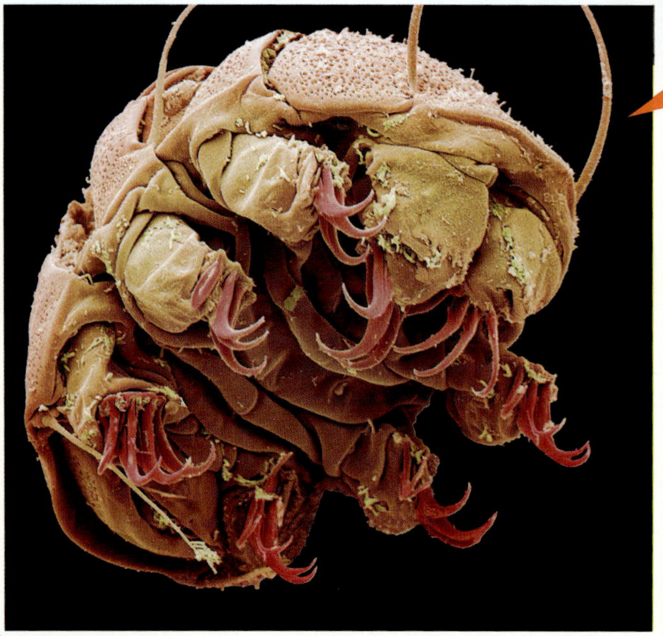

The tardigrade gets drier and smaller—like a shriveled-up raisin.

All the tardigrade's life processes shut down. It goes from walking, breathing, eating, and reproducing, and becomes a desiccated, or dried out, life form called a tun.

Years may pass by. In fact, the tun can stay in this death-like state for decades.

When a tardigrade becomes a tun, it is in a state called anhydrobiosis. This word means "life without water."

An SEM image of a tun

Eventually, however, rain falls or ice melts. Water surrounds the tun, and it rehydrates.

In less than an hour, the tardigrade goes back to its normal life. After years in suspended animation, it can walk, eat, and reproduce—as if nothing has happened!

Turning to Glass

All living things are made of tiny parts called cells. As a tardigrade starts to dry out, every cell in its body begins to lose water. Without water, cells can't survive.

However, a tardigrade has a unique, superhero-like adaptation.

Its cells start to make special proteins.

At first, the proteins are thick, like honey. They fill the tardigrade's cells.

Then, as the tardigrade gets drier and becomes a tun, the proteins turn to solid glass!

This glassy material protects the little animal's cells.

When the tun rehydrates, the glassy material dissolves into the water that's refilling the tardigrade's cells.

A tardigrade's body is made of about 1,000 cells. A human body contains 30 trillion cells.

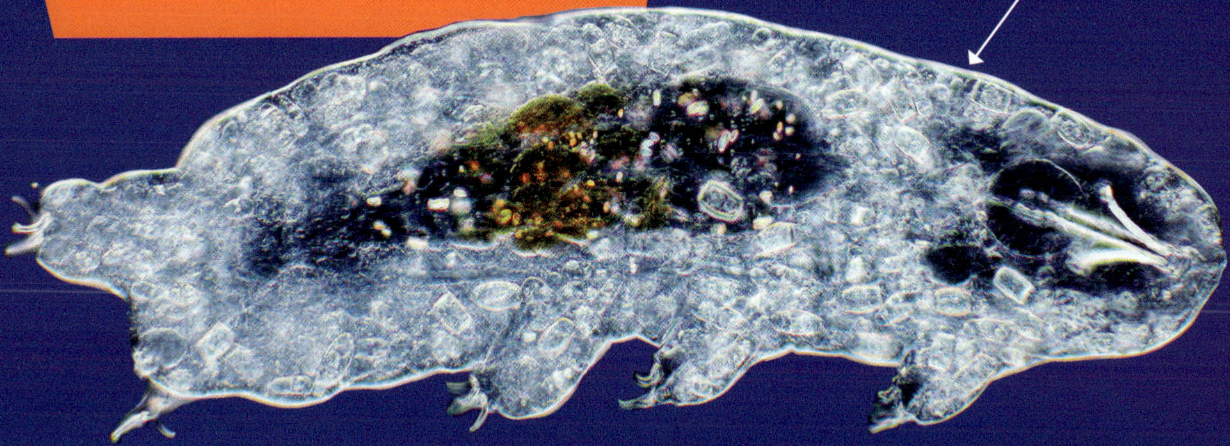

A tardigrade seen under a light microscope

That is amazing! So could a tardigrade survive as a tun for centuries? Or even forever?

That's a very cool idea! Scientists have considered it, but unfortunately they think it's unlikely.

Why Can't a Tardigrade Live Forever?

Once a tardigrade is in its tun state, the DNA in its cells may become damaged.

When a tardigrade is rehydrated, its body starts fixing any damaged DNA.

However, if the tardigrade has been a dried-out tun for a seriously long time, the DNA damage may be too great to fix. The little animal won't be able to survive.

DNA is a set of instructions inside the cells of living things. DNA tells cells how to look, work, and grow. DNA stands for deoxyribonucleic acid.

Earth's Superhero Survivors

Once a tardigrade is in its tun state, it becomes a superhero survivor.

To discover just how invincible tardigrade tuns are, scientists have subjected them to many extreme tests in laboratories.

Heating and Freezing

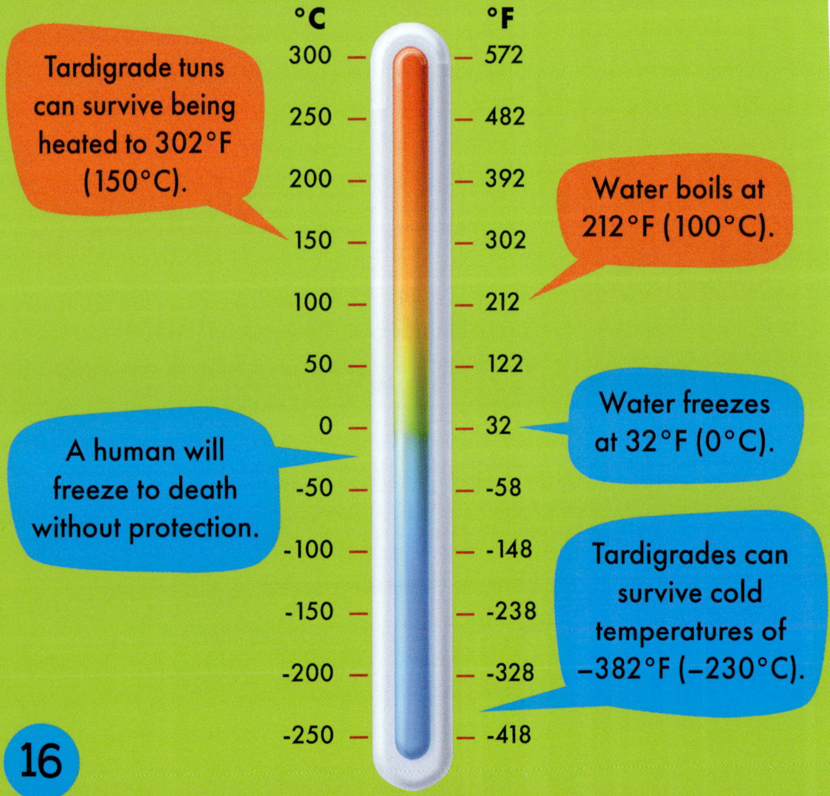

Blasted with Radiation

When we have X-rays in the hospital, a small amount of radiation is used to see inside our bodies and create pictures. Too much radiation, however, can be damaging to a living thing.

Tardigrades were blasted with 1,000 times the amount of X-rays that would kill a human—and they survived!

A tardigrade can survive losing up to 95% of the water in its body. If a human loses just 30%, they die!

When divers go deep under the ocean, all the water above them presses down on their bodies. This is called water pressure.

In the deepest part of Earth's oceans, the pressure would feel like 100 elephants on top of your head, pressing down on you. A human could not survive this pressure.

But—yep! You guessed it.

Tardigrade tuns were able to survive six times that amount of pressure!

High-Speed Impact? No Problem!

Scientists still had a question they wanted to answer. And tardigrades were the perfect candidates to take part in their experiment.

The Question

Could tiny life forms move from one planet to another on an asteroid or comet—and survive hitting their new home at high speed?

Some intrepid tardigrade pilots were prepared for this mission. They were frozen as tuns and placed into bullets inside a special gun.

Then, in a laboratory, the tuns were blasted from the gun into bags of sand—at about 2,000 miles per hour!

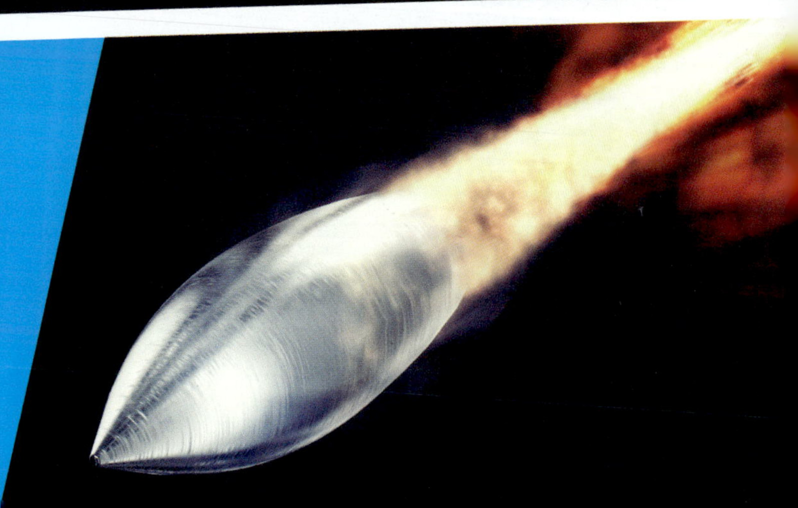

The Answer

It could be possible for a life form to survive a crash onto another planet. But only if it had tardigrade-like superhero survival skills.

The End of the World

Another team of scientists wanted to know if life on Earth could survive a catastrophic event. Perhaps a nearby star exploding or a giant asteroid hitting our planet.

$$P_{SN}(r,z) = \chi \int_{M_{min}}^{M_{max}} dm\, \xi(m) n_*(r,z) \tau^{-1}(m),$$

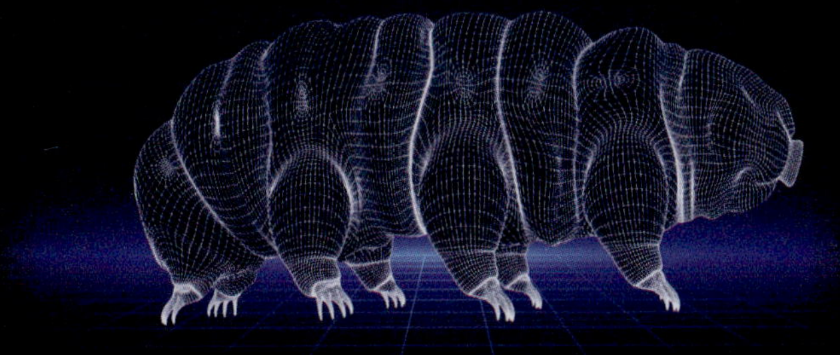

$$E = E_{GRB} \frac{\pi r^2}{\Omega d^2} = \frac{10^{62} r^2}{d^2}\ \mathrm{J}$$

The team used computers and super-complicated math. Their calculations showed that humans and most other living things would be wiped out. But tardigrades could survive the disaster and go on living.

To Boldly Go

Tardigrades are superhero-level survivors. What else can they do?

Space scientists wanted to know—could tardigrade tuns survive in space?

Let's do this!

Part of the International Space Station that's orbiting Earth

An astronaut wearing a protective suit during a space walk

Oxygen for breathing

All Earthlings, whether human or tardigrade, are designed to live within Earth's atmosphere. If a human is exposed to the dangers of space, they will be dead within two minutes!

What would happen to an astronaut without a spacesuit?

They would be blasted with radiation from the Sun and powerful cosmic radiation from our galaxy.

All the water in their body would boil.

The air would be pulled from their lungs.

They would suffocate from lack of oxygen.

In 2007, an unmanned spacecraft blasted into space. Inside a box on the outside of the craft was a brave crew of Tardi-Nauts.

Once outside of Earth's atmosphere, the box flipped open! The Tardi-Nauts were exposed to the dangers of space.

The spacecraft being prepared for launch

Space Dangers

Freezing cold
Powerful radiation
No oxygen
Very dry

After 10 days, the spacecraft returned to Earth. The Tardi-Naut tuns were taken to a laboratory and rehydrated. Sadly, the tardigrades exposed to space radiation did not survive their daring mission. But the rest of the crew did! They even went on to reproduce.

The Tardi-Nauts were inside these tiny chambers. Some of them were protected from radiation.

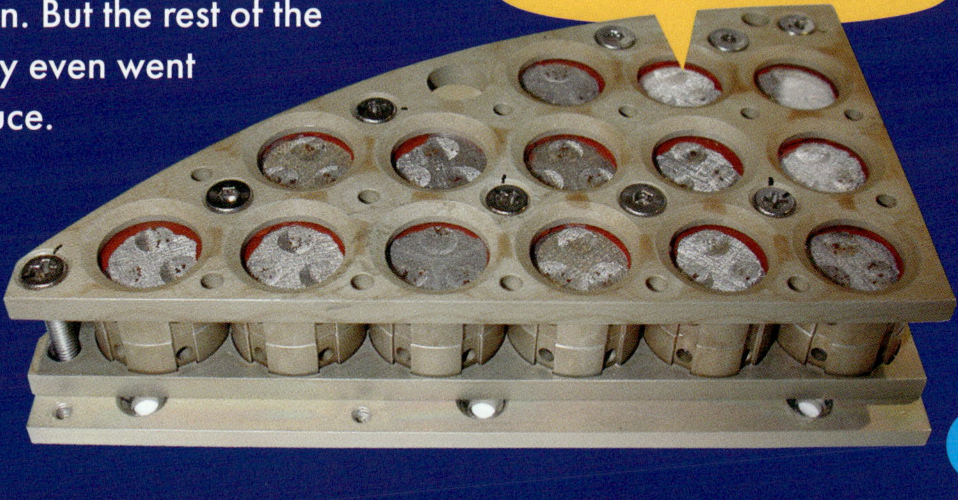

Being Cool Saves Lives

This is all so cool. But why are scientists experimenting with tardigrades?

Scientists want to know if the survival skills of tardigrades can help people in the future.

Every year, about 22 million children worldwide do not get the vaccines they need to protect them from deadly diseases.

Once vaccines leave a factory, they must be transported on ships and trucks. In the world's poorest countries, they may be delivered by motorcycle or on foot. At all times, the vaccines must be kept cold or they will spoil.

In some areas, clinics may not have electricity to power refrigerators for storing vaccines.

A health worker carrying vaccines in a cool box to a village in Ghana, Africa

Keeping vaccines cold is a major problem! But tardigrades could have the answer.

A vaccine is made of proteins. Scientists could combine tardigrade proteins with a vaccine and dry it out. The vaccine would then be protected—a little like a tardigrade tun. It could survive all kinds of temperatures and environments.

Once the vaccine arrived at its destination, it would be rehydrated and be ready to use.

This boy is receiving a polio vaccination.

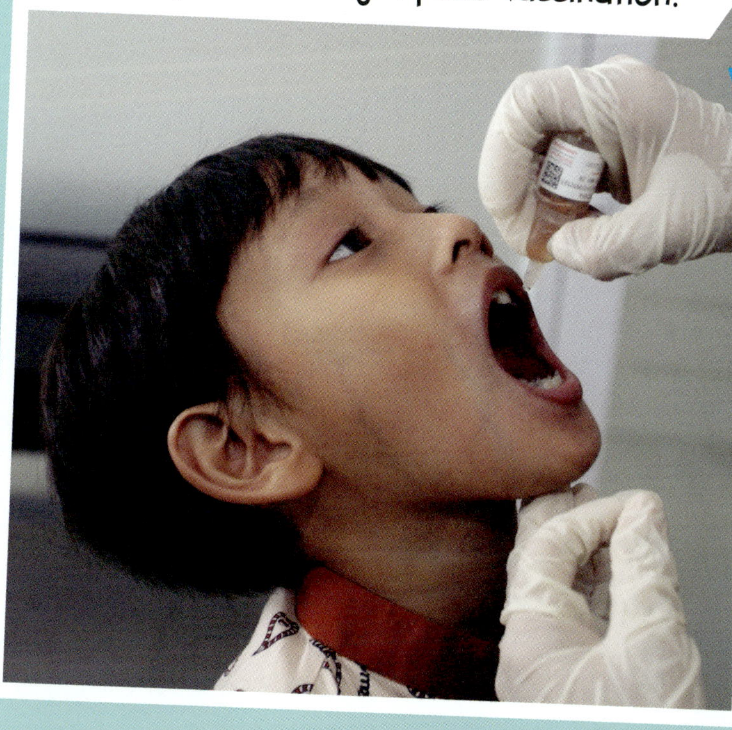

Wow! That is some super tardigrade science.

Indeed. And it could help save the lives of 1.5 million young children every year!

To Boldly Go—Again!

One day soon, astronauts will travel to Mars—or even farther away.

However, traveling and living in space is very damaging to the human body. The lack of Earth's gravity makes astronauts' bones and muscles grow weak. It can also damage a person's eyesight, balance, and heart.

Space travel exposes astronauts to harmful radiation from the Sun and outer space.

The frozen tardigrade tuns were in here.

In 2021, a team of Tardi-Nauts blasted off for a mission aboard the International Space Station (ISS). The Cell Science-04 mission would study how a tardigrade's body reacts to living in space.

International Space Station (ISS)

And remember how we said tardigrades can reproduce quickly? Some of the tardigrade crew reproduced while aboard the ISS. Then their young reproduced, and their young reproduced, and so on—to create four generations of space tardigrades.

ISS Commander Akihiko Hoshide studying tardigrades

The Tardi-Nauts were fed microscopic, plant-like algae on the ISS.

Finally, after two months, the tardigrade crew was sent back to Earth as tuns to be studied.

Scientists want to learn if tardigrades have special ways to protect their cells in space. They also want to discover if future generations are affected by their parents traveling to and living in space.

This knowledge might one day help scientists develop special treatments to protect human space travelers.

Superheroes in the Laboratory

Wow. These tiny good guys are just SO helpful!

You're right! And there are many other ways in which tardigrade survival skills could one day help us humans.

Surviving Drought

Scientists can study how tardigrades survive without water. Then they can use this knowledge to develop food crops that can survive without rain during droughts.

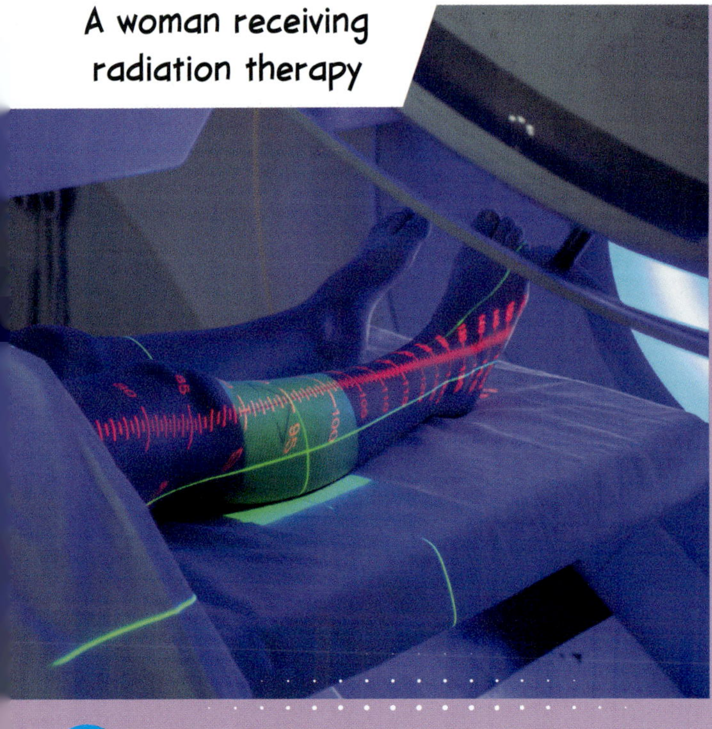

A woman receiving radiation therapy

Surviving Radiation

A tardigrade's cells are able to withstand high levels of radiation. People with cancer are sometimes treated with radiation therapy. Harmful cancer cells are blasted with radiation to kill them. However, healthy cells can be damaged, too.

Understanding how tardigrade cells survive radiation could make radiation therapy safer for people.

Tardigrade Sunscreen

A type of sunlight called UV light can be harmful to humans. We put on sunscreen to help block UV rays from reaching our skin.

Scientists have discovered a species of tardigrade that can survive damaging UV light. The tardigrade absorbs the harmful light. Then its body re-emits the light as a harmless, fluorescent, bright blue glow!

An illustration of a glowing blue tardigrade

The scientific team found a substance in the tardigrade that protects it. This substance could one day be used to make a new type of sunscreen for humans.

Out of This World!

That's a great theory! And scientists have thought about this. But sadly, the truth is probably a little more dull.

Along with the prehistoric ancestors of all animals, tardigrades first lived in the ocean. Once animals began to live on land, they had to survive dry times. Many animal groups adapted to have a waterproof skin so that their bodies did not lose water.

An Extreme World?

You might not think of a mossy log as an extreme habitat. But these tiny plants can quickly dry out during a heatwave. The ability to survive your home suddenly becoming dry is an essential skill for a tiny animal that lives in moss.

Tardigrades adapted to do survival their own way!

They evolved the ability to become a tun to survive without water. This superhero-like adaptation also helps them survive heating, freezing, and high-speed impacts.

A tardigrade's ability to fix its damaged DNA helps it withstand high doses of radiation, such as X-rays.

It might seem like tardigrades are alien beings. But we can be proud to say that these tiny, eight-legged heroes belong to planet Earth.

And they truly are Earth's Smallest Superheroes!

Glossary

algae

Plant-like living things. Most types of algae live in water.

atmosphere

A layer of gases surrounding a planet, moon, or star. Earth's atmosphere includes the gases nitrogen, oxygen, and carbon dioxide.

cell

A tiny part of a living thing. Humans are made of trillions of cells, while some living things, such as bacteria, are made of just one cell.

cuticle

A tough outer layer that protects the body of a tardigrade.

decade

A period of ten years.

DNA

A set of instructions inside the cells of living things that tells cells how to look, work, and grow. DNA stands for deoxyribonucleic acid.

fertilize

To make something, such as an egg, ready to grow and produce a new living thing.

fungi

Living things such as mushrooms, toadstools, molds, and yeasts.

generation

A group of people or animals that were born around the same time. You and your school friends are one generation. Your parents are a separate generation.

gravity

The force that causes objects to be pulled toward other objects. On Earth, gravity pulls everything down to the ground.

laboratory

A room, building, vehicle, or spacecraft where there is equipment that can be used to carry out experiments and other scientific studies.

moss

Tiny plants that grow close together in low masses that look a little like a green carpet.

near-microscopic

Too small to be seen with a person's eyes alone, but visible through a low-power home or school light microscope.

nutrients

Substances that are needed by living things to help them grow and stay healthy.

oxygen

A colorless gas in the air that is a natural part of Earth's atmosphere. There is also oxygen in water. Humans and animals need oxygen to breathe.

proteins

Building blocks in an animal or person's body. Proteins do specific jobs such as make muscles or build new cells.

radiation

A type of energy that travels through the air in invisible waves. Some types of radiation are helpful—for example, visible light from the Sun is radiation that allows us to see. But other types of radiation, such as X-rays or UV light from the Sun, can be harmful to people in large amounts.

rehydrate

To absorb, or soak up, water after getting dry, or dehydrating.

species

A type of living thing. The members of a species look alike and can reproduce together.

suspended animation

In an animal, all life processes stopping for a period of time—as if the animal has died.